WRINKLED WRAPPINGS

Sermons For Advent
And Christmas

JOHN R. BROKHOFF

CSS Publishing Company, Inc.
Lima, Ohio

Revised Edition
Copyright © 1975, 1995 by
CSS Publishing Company, Inc.
Lima, Ohio

Scripture quotations are from the *New Revised Standard Version of the Bible,* copyright 1989, by the Division of Christian Education of the National Council of the Churches of Christ in the USA. Used by permission.

Scripture quotations marked KJV are from the *King James Version of the Bible,* in the public domain.

Library of Congress Cataloging-in-Publication Data

Brokhoff, John R.
    Wrinkled wrappings : sermons for Advent and Christmas / John R. Brokhoff.
       p.   cm.
    ISBN 0-7880-0700-9
    1. Advent sermons. 2. Christmas sermons. 3. Sermons, American. I. Title.
BV4254.5.B76   1995
252'.61—dc20   95-4704
                                     CIP

This book is available in the following formats, listed by ISBN:
0-7880-0700-9 Book
0-7880-0701-7 IBM 3 1/2 computer disk
0-7880-0702-5 IBM 3 1/2 book and disk package
0-7880-0703-3 Macintosh computer disk
0-7880-0704-1 Macintosh book and disk package
0-7880-0705-X IBM 5 1/4 computer disk
0-7880-0706-8 IBM 5 1/4 book and disk package

PRINTED IN U.S.A.

To
The Rev. Robert W. Stackel, D.D.
"There is a friend who sticks closer than a brother."
(Proverbs 18:24)

Table Of Contents

Ready Or Not —
Here I Come!

Take ye heed, watch and pray: for ye known not when the time is. For the Son of man is as a man taking a far journey, who left his house, and gave authority to his servants, and to every man his work, and commanded the porter to watch. Watch ye therefore: for ye know not when the master of the house cometh, at even, or at midnight, or at the cockcrowing, or in the morning: Lest coming suddenly he find you sleeping. And what I say unto you I say unto all, Watch.

— Mark 13:33-37 (KJV)

When you were a child, did you play the game, Hide and Seek? If you did, you will remember that the person who was "it" closed his eyes while the rest went to hide. To give them time to hide, the child started counting: 5, 10, 15, 20 and up to 100. Then he would say, "Ready or not, here I come!" The point of the game was to hide oneself so well that the leader could not find you, for if he found you, and beat you back to the goal, you had to be "it" the next go-around. The secret of the game was preparing oneself against being found and caught. With excitement we heard the words, "Ready or not — here I come!"

In today's gospel lesson Jesus is saying to the world, "Ready or not — here I come." In chapter 13 of Mark, Jesus tells us that he will be returning to the earth "with great power and glory." As in the game, only it is not a game, there is a counting and an accounting going on right now. It is a count-down before the blast of his appearance on earth a second time to judge the world and to gather his faithful to himself. His coming may be soon, for the end of the world seems near. Though Russia and the United States agreed in 1974 to limit themselves to 2,500 nuclear missiles and bombers and permitted themselves to build an additional 1,200 missiles with multiple atomic warheads, by 1991 Russia had 10,877 and the U.S. had 11,602 nuclear weapons. Both sides have enough nuclear weapons to blow up the world not once but many times. While hundreds of millions are starving, nations spend annually $220 billion for arms. Leading ecologists warn us that we will suffocate ourselves with pollution. The world seems to be winding itself up. And we seem to know it, too. A cartoon shows a man wearing placards as he walks up and down the crowded streets of a big city. On the sign is the warning: "The end is nigh. Prepare to meet thy doom." The sign carrier says, "The horrible thing is that people don't laugh at me anymore!"

In our text Jesus is telling us to get ready for his second coming. The key word of our preparation is "Watch." He concludes his saying on this return with "And what I say unto you I say unto all, Watch." Ready or not, Jesus is coming. You'd better get ready! But how? In our text Jesus tells us what we need to do by way of preparation.

Watch And Wake Up

He tells us, first, to watch and wake up! The Greek word for "watch" literally means "chase sleep away." No one can watch and be asleep at the same time. If you are watching, you cannot be sleeping. Yet, this is a serious problem in our day. As Saint Francis said, many people are spiritually asleep. George Whitefield in his day felt the same about people, for he said, "The Christian world is in a deep sleep. Nothing but a loud voice can wake people out of it."

Of course, we sleep part of the time, about eight hours a night. But, this is not what Jesus meant when he said, "Lest coming suddenly he find you sleeping." "Sleep" is a symbolic word for a state of unpreparedness. It means that many of us don't care what happens to the world. Only when you are indifferent and unconcerned can you sleep. You know that when something is on your mind when you go to bed, you cannot sleep; you toss and turn all night long. You get up the next morning feeling as though you had not been to bed. Many just don't care what happens. The man on the street says, "I don't give a damn!" Another says, "What the hell do I care — Let the world go to the dogs!" That is the way Jonah felt about God's command to preach to Nineveh. In the middle of a storm at sea, Jonah was found fast asleep in the hold of the tossing ship. One of the things that hurt Jesus was, when he came back from praying in Gethsemane, he found his three closest friends asleep even though he asked them to watch and pray for him. In the parable of the virgins, five foolish virgins missed the bridegroom at midnight because they were asleep and allowed their lamps to go out. It is high time for us today to get awake with concern about the end of the world and Christ's return. "Wake, wake for the night is flying."

Today we need to get awake to the fact of Jesus' return to earth to bring history to a close, to judge the wicked, and to gather the faithful. There is no question about the certainty of his return. The only uncertainty is the time of his coming. Though religious fanatics seemed to know more than Jesus about the date of his coming, Jesus definitely says that only God knows the exact time of his coming again. Just because we do not know whether he will come tomorrow or 2,000 years from now does not say that he is not coming. As Christians Jesus has already come to us and we have accepted him by faith. At the end of our lives, he will come to us a second time and take us to himself in heaven. The hour of death is, in a sense, a second coming for a Christian. In addition, Jesus is coming in a cosmic sense. He will come at the end of the world. We believe this because Jesus said he would, and we have no good reason to doubt his promises. Through the ages the church has confessed, "From thence he shall come to judge the quick and the dead." Justice demands his return, because there must come a reckoning time. Reason calls for a settling of accounts. Evil must be destroyed and righteousness and truth must prevail. Satan cannot go on like this forever, and God is greater than Satan. The time must come when Satan is finally and for all time annihilated. The faithful need to be rescued and taken into the mansions of glory.

We need to get awake to Jesus' coming because Jesus tells us that his coming will be unexpected. Just as nobody knows when a thief is going to break into his home, so nobody knows when Jesus is coming again. If his coming is unexpected, then there is no time to prepare after he gets here. It is too late then. The time to prepare is before he comes, and since we do not know when he is coming, we must get ready now. If we are not awake, we cannot watch. If we do not watch, disaster will hit us. Some years ago a tragic accident took place north of Atlanta. A school bus was hit by a train at a crossing. Six little children were killed. In the investigation of the accident following the tragedy, it was reported that the watchman was not at the crossing but was warming himself in the caboose.

His coming will also be sudden. If he comes suddenly, there will be no time to prepare for him. This means that our readiness must be now lest he come all at once. A car accident can happen faster than a twinkling of an eye. An explosion occurs like a bolt in the blue. Birth pains hit a woman all at once. Jesus says his return will be like that — sudden, immediate! If we could see Jesus coming and his coming would take place in a year or so, or even a month from now, we might have time to get ready. But, that is not the case. You are ready now before he comes, or you will never be ready at his coming. So, it's time to wake up from your sleep of ho-hum, business-as-usual. He is coming — ready or not!

Watch And Pray!

We need not only to watch and wake up but also to watch and pray. Jesus says in our text, "Take ye heed, watch and pray . . ." You might be asking, "Now what in the world does prayer have to do with my readiness for Jesus' second coming?" It must have a lot to do with it or Jesus would never have urged us to pray as preparation for his coming.

Through prayer we keep in touch with God. Prayer is a means of communication. It is fellowship and conversation with God. If we daily keep in touch with God, we will not get careless about our lives. Living in God's presence will make us careful to live blameless lives, that when Jesus comes he will find us acceptable and presentable. When Eisenhower was president of the United States, he once visited Denver. His attention was called to a letter in the local newspaper saying that a six-year-old boy dying with cancer expressed a wish to see the president. One Sunday morning a black limousine pulled up in front of the boy's house. Ike stepped out of his car and knocked on the front door. The father, Donald Haley, opened the door wearing faded jeans, an old shirt, and a day's old beard. Standing behind him was the boy. Ike said, "Paul, I understand you want to see me. Glad to see you." Then he took the boy to the limousine to show it to him, shook hands, and left. The family and neighbors talked about the President's visit for a long time before the father always remembered it with regret because of the way he was dressed. He lamented, "What a way to meet the President of the United States." If we keep in fellowship with God through prayer, we will keep ourselves spiritually dressed for Christ's coming at any time.

We need to watch and pray as preparation for Jesus' coming again, because there are many people still without a knowledge of Christ. While waiting for Christ to come, we can spend our time profitably by praying for those who need to confess Christ as Lord and Savior. If Christ should return and people are without faith, think of the doom ahead for them. It is our privilege and responsibility to prepare them for Christ's return. A boy was once fishing with his grandfather in a boat off the coast. The lad noticed a flashing light from the lighthouse even though it was mid-day. The child said, "I thought they used the light only when there was a fog or a storm." His granddad replied, "No, son, they use it all the time. You can never tell when a fog or bad weather might come up. It's better to be prepared than to miss an opportunity to save someone's life." Prayer is an opportunity to save someone's soul. In good and bad times, in sunshine and storm we need to watch and pray that souls will respond to the love of God in Christ that they might be ready for the Lord's coming.

The early Christians watched and prayed by actually praying for Jesus to come back again. They said, "Maranatha," "Come, Lord Jesus, come quickly." They wanted Jesus to come back that accounts could be settled. There were hardships and persecutions of the faithful. Evil was rampant and the devil seemed to be loose in the world. They wanted Christ to come and put a stop to it. How far we are from the same concern and same condition in today's world? Have we not the right to pray for the same? Again, they prayed for Jesus' return because it meant their salvation. Unlike many of us the first Christians were not afraid of the Parousia. They wanted Jesus to come, for he was going to come for them and take them to heaven. This is known as the "rapture." It was a union of Christ and the believer, and Christ would gather his sheep and they would go into the kingdom of eternal life. This was the greatest thing that could happen to them. For those in Christ today, the end of the world and Jesus' coming do not mean judgment and condemnation but justification and vindication. Christ returns to rule and we who have faith in him shall rule with him. His victory is ours also. No wonder we are urged to get ready for his coming by praying.

Watch And Work!

Watch and wake up! Watch and pray! Here he comes — ready or not! You and I had better watch and work! In the parable of the text it says "to every man his work." What are we to do while waiting for Christ's return? Sit and twiddle our thumbs? Stand around and wait? This is what the first century Christians did. It became such a problem that Paul had to write, "He who does not work shall not eat."

When Jesus returns suddenly and unexpectedly, what will he find you doing? Will he find you with your guard down? Will he find you pilfering a money drawer? They say that the volcano which engulfed Pompeii came so suddenly that today they find the remains of people in the very act of doing their chores: baking, sewing, sweeping. When Jesus comes, will he find you taking a nap? Will he find you in sin like the husband who was on a trip to Bermuda with another woman and died from a heart attack?

Once John Wesley was asked what he would do if he knew this was his last day on earth. He replied, "At 4 o'clock I would have some tea. At 6 I would visit Mrs. Brown in the hospital. Then at 7:30 I would conduct a mid-week prayer service. At 10 I would go to bed and would wake up in glory." When Luther was asked what he would do on the day of Jesus' return, he said he would go out and plant a tree. Our text tells us that Christ expects each of us to be about our work so that when he comes, he will find us in gainful and constructive employment, taking care of the world as his trustees. Some years ago a tourist visited the Castle Villa Asconti along the shores of Lake Como in northern Italy. Only the old gardener opened the gates and the visitor stepped into the garden, which was perfectly kept. The visitor asked when the owner was last there. He was told, "Twelve years ago." Did he ever write? No. Where did he get instructions? From his agent in Milan. Does the master ever come? No. "But, you keep the grounds as though your master was coming back tomorrow." The old gardener quickly replied, "Today, sir, today."

A Christian watches and works as though the Master would return this very day. He wants Jesus to find him busy about his tasks: washing dishes, mending shoes, running a lathe, teaching school, planting a rose bush. Jesus will be pleased to see his faithful ones working hard to build a better world, a more Christian society.

Ready or not — here I come! That is what Jesus is saying to us today. If we are not now ready, we have reason to dread his coming. "Who can endure the day of his coming?" for he is coming to judge. On the other hand, if we are ready, we have reason to rejoice at the prospect of his coming today or tomorrow. He is coming to be with us, to bless us, to take us with him to glory. Then we will be like a mountaineer's wife. A preacher asked a man, "Are you ready for Judgment Day?" The mountaineer queried, "When is it comin'?" "Well,"

the preacher continued, "it might come today or tomorrow."
"For goodness sake, don't tell the missus," cautioned the
mountain man. "She'd want to go both days."

Good News
For Bad Times

Comfort, O comfort my people, says your God. Speak tenderly to Jerusalem, and cry to her that she has served her term, that her penalty is paid, that she has received from the Lord's hand double for all her sins.

A voice cries out: "In the wilderness prepare the way of the Lord, make straight in the desert a highway for our God. Every valley shall be lifted up, and every mountain and hill be made low; the uneven ground shall become level, and the rough places a plain. Then the glory of the Lord shall be revealed, and all people shall see it together, for the mouth of the Lord has spoken.

A voice says, "Cry out!" And I said, "What shall I cry?" All people are grass, their constancy is like the flower of the field. The grass withers, the flower fades, when the breath of the Lord blows upon it; surely the people are grass. The grass withers, the flower fades; but the word of our God will stand forever.

Get you up to a high mountain, O Zion, herald of good tidings; lift up your voice with strength, O Jerusalem, herald of good tidings, lift it up, do not fear; say to the cities of Judah, "Here is your God!" See, the Lord God comes with might, and his arm rules for him; his reward is with him, and his compense before him. He will feed his flock like a shepherd; he will gather the lambs in his arms, and carry them in his bosom, and gently lead the mother sheep.

— Isaiah 40:1-11

"Mail Early" is a slogan we often see and hear during these Advent days. The Postal Service would like the four billion Christmas cards sent annually in America in the mail by this second Sunday in Advent. American families send Christmas greetings costing an average of 35 cents per card plus a 32 cent stamp to send it. This amounts to a cost of $2.68 billion. That is a tremendous amount of money, time and trouble invested in just sending season's greetings to friends and families. What message could be worth that amount?

This is the season to send a message to each other. What are we saying on these Christmas cards in a period of bad times? Are we saying "Cheer up" or "Sorry about that misfortune" or with Job's wife, "Curse God and die"? Isaiah had this problem, too. When Deutero-Isaiah was called as we have it in Isaiah 40, he felt called to preach, but he did not know what to say to the world. He asked God, "What shall I cry?" These were bad times in Israel. For 50 years they had been in captivity in Babylon: despised people, displaced persons, disgruntled and discouraged. God called Isaiah in bad times to proclaim good news. God's message through Isaiah to us in similar bad times is the text for today. The good news for bad times is a message of comfort: "Comfort, O comfort my people, says your God."

Good News Of Pardon

There is, first of all, the good news of mercy. God tells Isaiah to tell the people and us, "Speak tenderly to Jerusalem ... her penalty is paid." This is good news for a people who have suffered a lot. The Israelites paid double for their sins. Before their captivity the Jews were faithless to God by worshipping and following other gods of the day. They practiced social injustice that made the rich richer and the poor poorer. They were guilty of gross immoralities. For 50 years they paid the price for their sins. They were captives of a foreign power and compelled to serve a hated people.

We Americans can identify with the ancient Israelites in Babylon. We have had it rough in recent years, too, because of our sins. Americans have left God for other gods — the gods of Wall Street, of Madison Avenue and of Pennsylvania Avenue. We put our trust in the power of money, stocks, and bonds and boasted of our national wealth. We have adored the god of Madison Avenue and rejoiced in the productivity of our factories resulting in a thing culture and a polluted environment. We have looked to the Great White Father in the White House and trusted that through laws and appropriations all of our national problems would be solved. Consequently, America has become a humiliated people and we are paying a horrible price for our sins. In the recent past, top government officials have had to leave office because of immoral conduct. We are beaten in a war which we were ashamed to admit was an immoral adventure. We thought we were absolutely self-sufficient, beholden to no other nation, and then found that our economy could be wrecked by an oil embargo initiated by Arab countries. We continue to face overwhelming drug problems, increasing racial tensions and unrest, crime, poverty, domestic violence, an AIDS epidemic, and the threat of terrorism from both home and abroad.

For a people in that condition, there is a message from God through our text. It is the good news that God will forgive our sins. This is the basic need of every person and nation. Realizing our sin, we cry from the depths of our beings the Kyrie Eleison, "Lord, have mercy upon us." God assures us that there is a balm in Gilead for those who repent and are weary of their sins. There is forgiveness with God. It is not God's will nor pleasure to condemn but to have mercy. As he said to the woman taken in adultery, Christ says to us as a people, "Neither do I condemn you. Go and sin no more."

Good News And Promise

God's Christmas-card message this Advent has another bit of good news for those bad times. It is news of warning and promise that he is coming to us. Isaiah is told to cry, "In the wilderness prepare the way of the Lord, make straight in the desert a highway for our God." When a people is in distress, God in concern comes to the people. When the Israelites were captive in Egypt, God heard their cries of misery. Now again, God hears the groaning of the people in Babylon. God knows

17

the plight we are in today, captives of our wicked ways, slaves to our sins.

But, do we take this promise seriously? Do we really believe it? In the classic movie, *Tora, Tora, Tora,* two young men are at their radar installation on a mountain guarding Pearl Harbor. On the screen is a large force of oncoming planes one early morning. They have never seen anything like this before. Excitedly they call headquarters and tell them about it. The officer does not take the report seriously. He thinks they are unnecessarily excited and that probably they see United States planes on patrol. He advises the radar spotters, "Well, don't worry about it." So they switched off their radar and went off to Sunday breakfast. In a little while a fleet of Japanese planes wrought havoc on Pearl Harbor. It all happened because of a tragic remark. "Well, don't worry about it!" Isaiah reports to us that God is coming to our world, and we say, "We have heard that before. Once more you are crying 'Wolf' and you have cried it too often. Don't worry about it." As a result of refusing to heed the warning, God is coming to judge the world, to punish evil-doers, and to gather his faithful to him. To treat this world from God lightly can spell doom to us. It can be a Pearl Harbor of the world.

God's coming can be good news in bad times for those who repent. Isaiah was told to get the world ready for God's coming by building a straight highway in the wilderness of sin. For God to come and save us, we must get straight with God. In today's wilderness of sin we have been living crooked lives. Crime is increasing 11 times faster than the growth of the American population. Murder, rape, armed robbery, and breaking and entering are significantly higher in the U.S. than in other industrialized nations (Japan, Sweden, France, and Austria). In one year alone shoplifting in the Emory campus bookstore cost over $15,000. It seems that none of us can do what is right. All of us sin and come short of what God expects of us. We are like the man who appeared once again before a judge who said, "I've had you up here for speeding, drunken driving, reckless driving, parking alongside fire hydrants, driving a car without a license plate, and the last time you were here I ordered your driver's license suspended. What's the charge this time?" The defendant mumbled, "Jay-walking, your Honor."

The way to get straight with God as preparation for God's coming is to repent. It means to stop sinning and start walking on the straight path of righteousness. When are we going to do this? For my birthday a daughter sent me a humorous card of a Hippie carrying a sign, "Repent." On the inside the card continued, "Tomorrow (today's your birthday! Have a happy one!)" That is the way most of us want it to be: repent, yes, but let's wait until tomorrow and then tomorrow never comes. If we are going to escape the judgment of God and if we want to be accepted by God as one of the faithful, we must repent — today!

Good News Of Security

The good news for bad times continues. The good news that comforts is the news of security. God tells us through Isaiah in our text that "all people are grass ... the grass withers, the flower fades; but the word of our God will stand forever."

It is a fact of life that, as a popular hymn puts it, "Change and decay [are] in all around I see." The only thing that is certain is uncertainty. Like grass which is here today and gone tomorrow, life is transient. You and I change. Our customs and even our morals change. We do not have the same attitudes we once had. Life is short. You realize this fact when you hit age 50. Then you realize that you do not have as many years to live as you once had. Before you know it, you will be gone. Return to a community after a year and you can hardly recognize the place: old places have been removed and new houses built. The stock market changes daily and in a year can lose half of its strength while millions lose billions of dollars. In days of economic uncertainty many are not sure they will have a job tomorrow.

All of this adds up to a deep sense of insecurity. What is permanent? Is there anything safe and secure? The world keeps seeking for a place that is secure from conquest or theft. A two-hour drive out of New York City along the Hudson River will bring you to what is called the safest place in the world. It is an underground vault in Iron Mountain. It was once an abandoned mine. Beneath 200 feet of solid rock, vaults are built lined with steel and concrete. It is considered safer than Fort Knox. Many New York banks store their most valuable papers there. Though this may be considered safe, it is also subject to change and conquest.

There is only one thing that is absolutely safe and secure. It is the Word of God. This is according to the message Isaiah has in our text. "The word of our God will stand forever." The Word is as sure and certain as God himself, for the Word is God. No worldly affair, no outward circumstance, no time change can remove or diminish the Word of God. It is the focal and eternal point of time and eternity. God's truth in the Word, which is the Bible, is everlasting truth. What was true a million years ago will be true a million years from now. The Word of God contains the promises of God, and they are true and dependable. What God says, God always accomplishes and fulfills. For ages God promised a Messiah and in a few weeks the Christian world will be celebrating God's fulfillment of the promise in the Babe of Bethlehem. God's values in the Word — the moral standards — will never, never change. We say this in spite of changing moral values in our day and the new morality. God's commands are for every generation as long as time lasts. Woe to that person who disregards and disobeys them! He will fall on a rock and be crushed.

It is good to say this and it sounds good, but it is meaningless to you and me unless we possess the Word of God in our lives. If we do not believe and accept the truth of the Word of God, we cannot be the recipients of the good news of our security in God's Word. This means we must believe, accept, and have deep convictions that the truths of God's Word are really true and binding. This is one of our problems today;

we lack deep convictions of the truth. In a study of 1,580 Protestant clergymen some years ago it was revealed that 33 percent of them are not certain of God's existence; 29 percent are not sure of Christ's deity; 31 percent do not believe acceptance of Christ is necessary to be saved. These convictions, the book says, are shared equally by the laity. If we are going to have a sense of certainty and security in our lives in these changing times, we must have deep and abiding convictions based on God's Word. We must know what to believe and why we believe what we believe. Then God will be in the midst of us and we shall not be moved, as certain and solid as the rock of Gibraltar. He who puts his trust in God's Word will find stability for his life.

Good News Of Hope

There is comfort for God's people because of the good news of hope. Isaiah calls to us: "Here is your God!" God will come with strength, and in love he will gather his people to him like a shepherd. We like sheep have gone astray, but God will come and gather us again to himself. This is the good news of hope.

When times like these are bad, we tend to lose hope that things turn out all right. The American people are presently in a state of cynicism and pessimism. The fad is to downgrade everyone and everything. In a cartoon in the *Wall Street Journal* two elderly people are seated across from each other in their living room. The man says, "True. We *do* eat right; we *do* get plenty of exercise; we *have* our health which *is* the main thing. But, I *still* say to hell with everything." As a humorous Christmas gift, a pastor gave his friends a diploma from a phony university awarding the degree of Doctor of Phantasmagoria. It was signed by the chairman of the board: "Don Giveadam (Don't Give a Damn)." A study was made of changes that have taken place in college students across the country. One of the major changes reported was a general dissatisfaction, apathy, and malice among them. They feel frustrated by the demonstrations of the '60s and now feel loneliness, anxiety, and frustration. It is a generation without hope.

Is there any basis for hope for our time? To be sure, there is no hope in man, only in God. Once again we need to lift our heads to the heavens and hear, "Behold your God!" God is greater than man and our problems. This is God's world and God holds the world in God's hands. God is God and the ultimate victory is God's. We can live today in hope because we are on God's side in this conflict and God will see us through. With God we can never be in a hopeless situation. There is hope for a better world because Christ is the answer to these problems. This applies to any problem you can mention. There is no problem that cannot be solved when the problem is approached in the spirit of Christ — a spirit of justice, love, and goodwill.

And there is hope for you as an individual. One thing is sure: you need not stay as you are. You can change by the power of God's Spirit. God in Christ can overrule in God's providence and bring the best out of the worst in you. Surrender your heart to Christ and submit to God's will. Then you will see in your life an almost immediate change for the better.

This is the message on God's Christmas card you are getting this Advent. Are you interested in the message or just the card? An elderly couple was in a card shop looking for Christmas cards. The wife said, "Here is one I like but I don't care for the words." Her husband replied, "That doesn't matter, because nobody bothers to read the message anyway." Maybe the world — you and I — feel the same about God's message on the Christmas card. We want the trappings, the music, the Santa, the good times of Christmas but not the message. Yet, it is the message that is all-important, for it is a message of good news in bad times.

You Don't
Need Jesus

There was a man sent from God, whose name was John. He came as a witness to testify to the light, so that all might believe through him. He himself was not the light, but he came to testify to the light.

This is the testimony given by John when the Jews sent priests and Levites from Jerusalem to ask him, "Who are you?" He confessed and did not deny it, but confessed, "I am not the Messiah." And they asked him, "What then? Are you Elijah?" He said, "I am not." "Are you the prophet?" He answered, "No." Then they said to him, "Who are you? Let us have an answer for those who sent us. What do you say about yourself?" He said, "I am the voice of one crying out in the wilderness, 'Make straight the way of the Lord,' " as the prophet Isaiah said.

Now they had been sent from the Pharisees. They asked him, "Why then are you baptizing if you are neither the Messiah nor Elijah, nor the prophet?" John answered them, "I baptize with water. Among you stands one whom you do not know, the one who is coming after me; I am not worthy to untie the thong of his sandal." This took place in Bethany across the Jordan where John was baptizing.

— John 1:6-8, 19-28

The man the world needs now. Who is he? A wise man like Socrates? A military genius like Alexander? A brain like Einstein? A statesman like Lincoln? A theologian like Barth? Jesus? No, the man the world needs now is not Jesus. Are you shocked at this? Do you call it heresy? If the world does not need Jesus, then whom does it need? The man the world needs even more than Jesus is John the Baptist! If Jesus came without the work of John the Baptist, the world would not know, appreciate, or accept Jesus as Lord and Savior. It was necessary for someone to prepare the world that when Jesus came, he might be accepted. The season of Advent is a period of preparation for the coming of Christ at Christmas or at the end of time, and John the Baptist's ministry is the central theme of the season.

God knew that the world needed someone to prepare humankind for God's Son. That is why our text says, "There was a man sent from God, whose name was John." Through a miraculous birth, John the Baptist was sent by God with a mission to ready the world for Christ. John the Baptist himself understood his purpose and who he was. Our gospel lesson for today tells how John was asked who he was. He was honest to say that he was not the Christ, the prophet, or Elijah. He knew that he was sent to witness to Christ. Our text explains the work of John: "He came as a witness to testify to the light, so that all might believe through him."

I Am A Voice

Before you can have Christ, you must first confront John the Baptist who will prepare you to receive the Christ. John the Baptist is the man the world needs now because he is the voice of God crying in the wilderness of our world. When he was asked by the religious leaders of his day, "Who are you?" he replied, "I am the voice of one crying out in the wilderness, 'Make straight the way of the Lord.' "

It was a voice making people realize their need of a Savior. Before you want a Savior, you must be convinced that you are a sinner in need of someone to save you. John the Baptist made the people of his day aware of their sins. In his preaching by the Jordan River, he exposed and condemned the sins of his day. He was a very uncomfortable figure. Someone who points out your sins is always an uncomfortable fellow to have around. He looked the message of repentance that he delivered. His very being was a protest to the luxury and laxity of the day. He was a wild-looking figure living in the open country,

24

dressed in an animal's skin, and eating locusts and wild honey. In fiery, frank, and forceful language he condemned the sin of the day and called people to turn from their wickedness. He threatened them with the damnation of hell-fire. He said that the axe was at the trunk of the tree and every evil tree would be cut down and thrown into the fire.

You know, we need a John the Baptist for these years. Paradoxically we are living in the most sin-saturated society with the least consciousness of our sin. It caused Menninger to write a book titled, *Whatever Became of Sin?* Sin is no longer sin to modern man. There is sin, of course, but we call it a disease or a crime. Maybe it is a neurosis or a social maladjustment.

To Sin Is Human

What are we doing about our sin? We are accepting it as a normal way of life. We keep saying that "Everybody's doing it — why shouldn't I?" Sin is popular in our day. Without it life would be dull and boring. Several years ago someone got the idea of starting a fad of wearing SIN buttons (Stop Inflation Now), and the public took instantly to it. Bumper stickers appeared, "Honk if you want to sin." We seem to be unconcerned about sinning, because we feel that it is human to err. A salesman was showing a lady various alligator handbags. She found a defect in every one. In desperation the salesman said, "Madam, if there were not a defect, it would not be an alligator." So, we expect to sin, and we take it in our stride. If we are caught in our sin, we are not sorry that we did it. We are just sorry that we were caught. You know how it is: You get a ticket for speeding and after the patrolman leaves, you don't have tears of remorse, but you berate yourself for not having watched the rear-view mirror more closely. And since we accept sin as a fact of life, we try to control it if it gets out of hand. We are prone to legalize our sin. When gambling gets so popular that we cannot control it, we legalize gambling and get taxes from it. Several states have lotteries and many people play the lottery. The U.S. has 22,520,000 marijuana users so a movement continues to push for the legalization of the smoking of marijuana. At one time a convention of youth in California called for the legalizing of prostitution. If we can't stop a sin, we shrug our shoulders, accept it as a fact of life, and make it acceptable by legalizing it.

If we do not accept sin as a way of life, we deny it. We actually claim that we do nothing wrong. When a public figure was having trouble with the press, she said, "I have never done anything wrong in my life. I wasn't even sent to the principal's office when I was in school." There are many who do not feel as though anything is wrong in their lives. In front of a house where there were many crutches on the front porch, a little girl was crying because she was not invited to the party. A passerby asked her what the trouble was. She explained, "There's a party in there for handicapped children — and I can't go in because there's nothing the matter with me." You may kid yourself about not having any sin but not only God knows better but all the rest of us do. In response to an evangelist's sermon, a man got up and confessed, "I've been a sinner, a contemptible sinner. And I've been one for years, but I never knew it before tonight." A deacon in the aisle whispered to him, "Sit down, brother, the rest of us have known it all the time."

If we do not deny that we sin, we try to hide it. This has been man's custom from the very first. After disobeying God in the Garden, Adam and Eve made themselves aprons of fig leaves to hide the fact they lost their innocence. When God came to them, they hid behind the trees as God called, "Adam, where are you?" The great king, David, was a master at covering up his sin. After his adultery with Bathsheba, he tried to cover it up by having her husband murdered while he was fighting in the front lines. He seemed to have hid it successfully except he did not hide it from God who sent Nathan to say to him, "Thou art the man." Don't we do the same? We cover our footprints. We wear gloves to prevent fingerprints. To cover one lie, we tell another and another. We appear to be good and we pose with a false veneer of piety when we are as guilty as hell underneath. But, it is all so foolish, for murder will out! What is whispered in the secret closet will one day be shouted from the housetops.

What does John the Baptist tell us to do about our sin? He calls upon us to do the only right thing a man can do when he sins. That is to repent. This is a common word that is used so often that it has become meaningless. It means that we come to the point that we have deeply grieved and offended God. We recognize that we are helpless and hopeless in our sins. In our lost condition we cry out, "My sins, Oh my sins!" We ask with Paul, "Who will deliver me from this body of death?" To repent is to make an about-face, from sin to goodness, from Satan to God, from self to Christ. It means a whole new way of life, a radical change in lifestyle. An alcoholic lost his business. Through AA he conquered the habit and started up a real estate business. He named his company, "Rebos" for "sober" spelled backwards. Through this name, he wanted to ever remind himself that he had to make an about-face in his life at least as far as alcohol was concerned.

It is at this point of repentance that new life begins both for the individual or a nation. In his book, *From Under The Ruins,* Solzhenitsyn says, "Only through the repentance of a multitude of people can the air and the soil of Russia be cleansed, so that a new, healthy national life can grow up."

I Am A Finger

It is this voice of John the Baptist that the world needs now so that it might confess its sins and repent. But, the world needs more than this voice. It needs a finger pointing to the solution of sin. John the Baptist is that finger which points to Jesus as the Christ, the Savior from sin. In our text he tells his people that there stands one among them they do not know. He tells them that this one will baptize with the Spirit. As Jesus approaches John cries out, "Here is the Lamb of God who takes away the sin of the world!" John was not the Christ; he was only the witness to Christ, telling the world that he was the one who was the answer to their sins.

27

This is what our world needs, because we have been dealing symptomatically with the problem of evil in our society. We have been trying to make men good by drugs, imprisonment, and even rewards to attain behavior modification. For a time we were told that education would make men decent. Then we put confidence in passing laws. Better housing was supposed to be the answer. Then we espoused the cause of civil rights. None of these ever got to the heart of the problem. At one time a congregation in Michigan held a television bonfire after the evening service. The members were so angry and disgusted with television programs that sets worth $1,400 were thrown into the fire. What did the poor helpless television sets have to do with the kind of programs that are shown? Of course, nothing was wrong with the sets. It was with the men who planned and produced the programs. It is like a man praying every Wednesday in the prayer meeting asking God to clear out the cobwebs of sin in his life. One man got tired of hearing the same prayer week after week. He interrupted the prayer to say, "Don't do it, God. Don't do it! Don't clear out the cobwebs. Kill the spider!"

John the Baptist is the man we need today to tell us that the only solution to sin is Jesus Christ. He is the finger that points to Christ as the Lamb of God who takes away the sin of the world. All sin is against God and only God can take it away by forgiveness. And God did this by coming in Jesus of Nazareth at Christmas. God identified with humans, becoming sin, and bearing the sins of humankind for all time. His death on the cross was the perfect sacrifice for the sins of the world. This is what Christmas is really all about. He was the fulfillment of God's promise to send a Messiah to deliver the world. His name indicated his mission, for "Jesus" means "He shall save." The angels told the shepherds, "For unto you is born this day in the city of David a Savior who is Christ the Lord." Jesus was born to die. The cradle and the cross are two sides of a coin. This is according to God's wonderful plan of salvation. It is not God's will for anyone to perish and go to hell, but it is his desire that everyone be saved and have life. The wonderful good news is that Christ did die for our sins. The way has been opened for repentant sinners to return to God and find acceptance, forgiveness, and love. Because of Christ man has freedom at last — freedom from self, Satan, and sin. The way is open to a full, free life in Christ. Now, brother, that's what you call "good news"!

All of this witnessing by John the Baptist is wonderful. But the question remains why there is still so much sin in the world, more than ever it seems. We ask why, if what we said is true, there is so much guilt in the world. People are generally not happy and they live in misery caused by sin. What the world needs is a John the Baptist to witness to Christ as Savior. This has become the privilege and responsibility of Christians. A true Christian will witness daily to Christ as Lord and Savior. Apparently we are failing in witnessing to Christ. The percentage of U.S. citizens who claim membership in Protestant churches continues to decline and by the year 2000 it will represent only 34 percent of the population. In this century one-third of those received into the church have fallen away. Some churches suggested a moratorium on sending missionaries overseas. One church reduced its missionaries by 43 percent and another church dropped the number of its missionaries by 62 percent in a period of ten years. Once again, however, the church is beginning to get interested in witnessing through evangelism. At a world convocation on evangelism held in Jerusalem several years ago, a final message said, "Every Christian is summoned to be an evangelist. We believe that one true function of the ordained minister is to train Christians for person-to-person witness ..."

What and when and how to witness often calls for wisdom from God. Misplaced witnessing — "Are you saved?" can turn people off Christ. The foolproof way of witnessing is the quality of your daily life. A true Christian is a sermon without words. Bishop John Selwyn once found it necessary to rebuke a candidate for baptism in Melanasia. The candidate violently slapped the bishop on the face. Though the bishop was heavier than the candidate, the bishop just crossed his arms and waited to see if he would be struck again. This unnerved the attacker and he ran off. Years later the bishop returned to England. The same native came to another missionary for baptism. When he was asked in what name he wanted to be baptized, he replied, "Call me John Selwyn, for it was he who first taught me what Christ is like."

Really the world today does not need Christ. It needs John the Baptist to call men to repent and to point to Christ as Savior. Indeed, men everywhere desperately need Christ, but to get to Christ we need first to go through John the Baptist who convinces us of our need for Christ. Christ is the ultimate of our lives and John is the penultimate. To get the ultimate, we must first pass through the penultimate. During this Advent season John the Baptist confronts us with our sins that we might find a Savior on Christmas. God sent John for this purpose — thanks be to God!

You're Going To
Have A Baby!

In the sixth month the angel Gabriel was sent by God to a town in Galilee called Nazareth, to a virgin engaged to a man whose name was Joseph, of the house of David. The virgin's name was Mary. And he came to her and said, "Greetings, favored one! The Lord is with you." But she was much perplexed by his words and pondered what sort of greeting this might be. The angel said to her, "Do not be afraid, Mary, for you have found favor with God. And now, you will conceive in your womb and bear a son, and you will name him Jesus. He will be great, and will be called the Son of the Most High, and the Lord God will give to him the throne of his ancestor David. He will reign over the house of Jacob forever, and of his kingdom there will be no end." Mary said to the angel, "How can this be, since I am a virgin?" The angel said to her, "The Holy Spirit will come upon you, and the power of the Most High will overshadow you; therefore the child to be born will be holy; he will be called Son of God. And now, your relative Elizabeth in her old age has also conceived a son; and this is the sixth month for her who was said to be barren. For nothing will be impossible with God." Then Mary said, "Here am I, the servant of the Lord; let it be with me according to your word." Then the angel departed from her.

— Luke 1:26-38

During a pastoral call, a three-year-old boy climbed in the lap of a pastor and whispered confidentially, "I know a secret!" The pastor asked, "Will you tell me your secret?" "Yes," the little fellow giggled delightedly, "but you mustn't tell my mamma." When the pastor promised not to tell, the boy continued, "My mamma's going to the hospital to have a baby. But don't tell her. Me and Daddy want her to be surprised!"

Would you be surprised if someone told you that you were going to have a baby? The men and children here this morning would say, "That lets me out!" Women over 50 would say, "Who do you think you are kidding?" When an angel came to the Virgin Mary, it was a surprise when he told her that she was to have a baby. The fact is that regardless of sex or age, every one of us is going to have a baby this Christmas!

If we understood the real meaning of Christmas, we would not be surprised to learn that "You are going to have a baby." What does Christmas mean to you? A Gallup poll indicates that 35 percent of those interviewed said they considered Christmas a religious festival. Twenty-six percent thought of it as a holiday; 23 percent considered it an opportunity to meet family and friends; five percent looked at Christmas as a time for eating and drinking; 11 percent had no opinion. In other words, 65 percent of the people do not understand the true meaning of Christmas. As a religious festival Christmas is more than Santa, more than a celebration of a past event, more than exchanging gifts, more than a story about shepherds, angels, a manger, and wise men. The true meaning of Christmas is that Christ is to be born or re-born in us on Christmas Day. The gospel lesson for this fourth Sunday in Advent is a birth announcement. A messenger from God comes to each of us today with the good news, "You're going to have a baby!"

Are You Troubled?

How do you react to this announcement, "You're going to have a baby"? What should your reaction be as a true Christian? How did the Virgin Mary react? Our text shows what your reaction ought to be.

Like Mary, you can be troubled about the announcement. Our text says, "She was much perplexed by his words." The announcement of becoming a mother can be very disturbing. It can be shocking and traumatic. Yet, this announcement is not an uncommon experience. More than 300,000 in the world get this message daily, for this many babies are born each day.

Some married women are troubled by the news that they are pregnant, because they do not want another baby. Their reaction may be, "Oh, no, not another! We can't afford another child!" Some go to an abortion clinic demanding an end to the pregnancy.

It can be a troublesome message to unwed girls. In the United States 98 out of 1,000 teenagers get pregnant annually outside of wedlock. This is the result of the fact that so many of American teenagers have pre-marital sex experiences. And are they troubled when they get the message, "You're going to have a baby"? The unwed prospective mother wonders when and how she can tell her boyfriend and what he will say and do about it. How can she tell her parents? Because of fear, she postpones telling them until she no longer can hide her pregnancy. She is troubled about her schooling. Should she get married? Put the child up for adoption? Get an abortion? "You're going to have a baby" can be the worst news for an unmarried girl. But, it could be the best news, if when she told her parents she was pregnant and was asked, "Who is the father?" she, like the Virgin Mary, could answer, "God."

Mary was troubled when the angel greeted her with the announcement. Mary was upset because of the appearance of an angel. It was a strange voice, one she never heard before. She was troubled by his greeting, "Greetings, favored one! The Lord is with you." Who could this be? A ghost? The devil? Could this be God? The newness and strangeness of the experience was unsettling to this teenaged girl. She asks, "What's it all about?"

If each of us is going to have a baby this Christmas, we too can be troubled. If Christ is to be born in us, we have the same reaction as the Virgin Mary. Instinctively we ask, "Who am I? What did God find in me that he would humble himself to be born in me?" As the centurion said to Jesus, "I am not worthy to have you come to my house." Look, Lord, I am a sinner, I am not fit to be a carrier of you. The carol is right when it says, "Cast out our sin, and enter in." With this sense of unworthiness we hear the announcement of our having a baby with troubled hearts.

33

Are You Afraid?

Like Mary, we can react with fear. Our text says, "Do not be afraid, Mary." It was natural for the Virgin Mary to be afraid of becoming a mother. As a typical human being, she was afraid of the consequences of being an unwed mother. She knew she would have to face the gossip of the community in which she lived. She would be an object of shame and disgrace. People would look down upon her and tell all kinds of nasty stories about her. Moreover, she was afraid of what her fiance, Joseph, would do. He would have the right to divorce her, according to the law. She could not stand the thought of losing him, because she deeply and dearly loved him. She could not wait for the day when they were to be married, and she often told him that she could not live without him. She was madly in love with him, and what would he think of her if she became pregnant? Mary had a real reason to be afraid of the announcement that she was to be a mother, because the law of her day called for an adulteress to be stoned to death. You remember that when Jesus was a man, a woman caught in the act of adultery was about to be stoned by religious leaders. To consent to being an unwed mother would mean Mary was putting her life on the line. If you were Mary, wouldn't you be afraid, too?

Although modern society seems to take unwed motherhood in its stride, barely lifting an eyebrow or uttering a word of criticism, many unwed mothers take their pregnancy with anxiety. They are afraid that they will have to drop out of school or they will lose their jobs. Their parents may disown them and turn them out. Their reputations will go down the drain. Most of all, they fear a loss of self-respect. How can they live with themselves in the future? This fear serves many as a deterrent to getting pregnant before marriage.

The Virgin Mary, however, had a healthy fear when the angel came with the announcement, "You are going to have a baby." It was a fear in terms of awe, reverence, and respect in the presence of a holy one, an angel, a messenger from

God. This is a normal reaction when people step into the real presence of the Holy. The angel said to the shepherds, "Do not be afraid, I am bringing you good news of great joy." When Jesus and the disciples were on the top of the Mount of Transfiguration and they heard God speak, the disciples fell on their faces before the transfigured Christ. He said to them, "Get up and do not be afraid." God is holy, the totally other, and humans are sinful and unworthy to be in the presence of the Almighty. We often express a desire to be in the presence of God, but if God actually confronted us, we probably would be scared to death. It is like a certain man who did not have all of his senses. It was his custom each evening to go to the barn, take off his cap, and say, "Howdy, Lord." Then he would deliver a sermon. Some friends decided to play a trick on him. They hid in the hay loft and when Jake said, "Howdy, Lord," they answered, "Howdy, Jake." Thinking it was the voice of God, he dropped his hat, ran away as fast as he could, and never again did he come back to preach.

The solution to this fear is what the angel said to Mary, "You have found favor with God." If God is a God only of justice and wrath, you and I need to be afraid of God. But, God comes to us personally and wants to be born in us because God loves us. God accepts us and makes us God's children. God comes not to harm, not to condemn but to bless and save us. Yes, we shall always fear God in terms of reverence and awe, but we never need to be afraid of God, for God loves us with God's whole being.

Are You Curious?

Like Mary, in the third place, we can react with curiosity about this announcement. "You're going to have a baby." After the angel told Mary that she was to be the mother of a son and his name was to be Jesus, she responded naturally with the question, "How can this be, since I am a virgin?" That is a good question, isn't it? How can a woman have a baby without having intercourse with a man? Gabriel explained to Mary that the father of her child would be the Holy Spirit. To this day we confess in the Creed, "conceived by the Holy Ghost, born of the Virgin Mary." No man can take credit or be blamed for impregnating Mary. In a church Christmas pageant, Mary and Joseph were asking for a room in the inn. The innkeeper asked, "Can't you see the 'No vacancy' sign?" Joseph replied, "Yes, but can't you see that my wife is expecting a baby any minute?" The innkeeper retorted, "Well, that's not my fault." Joseph responded, "Well, it's not mine, either!"

Though it is a controversial subject among many, the virgin birth is an important doctrine in the church. It does not teach that the virgin birth makes Jesus sinless. It does not mean that normal sexual relations and childbirth are sinful. The church has always taught the virgin birth because of the truth that Jesus' birth was totally the work of God. Man had no part in it. Jesus is God's creation, God's son, God's child. This makes Jesus unique among humans. From the time of the original creation the Spirit has been and still is the creative agent. The Spirit created Jesus in the womb of Mary.

"How can this be?" is the question of every person who is told that Jesus is to be born in him. When Sarah was age 90 she laughed when she was told that she was to have a child. She too asked, "How can this be?" Jesus told Nicodemus, a teacher of Israel, that he must be born again to enter the Kingdom. He asked, "How can this be? Must a man re-enter the womb of his mother?" The problem confronts us this Christmas. If Christmas is to mean anything at all, Christ is to be born in each of us in the same way Mary conceived. It is by the Spirit. It seems as impossible for us to be born anew as it was for Mary to have a child without a husband. The angel reminds us, as did Mary, that with God all things are possible. It does seem impossible that I, as old, as ugly, as dirty as I am, can be a new person by having Christ born in me. To have Christ born in me is to have a new life, a new world, a new creation, a new spirit, and a new attitude. All of life is different. It is another world, like being born all over again as another person. If Christ is born in us, we have the spirit of Christ in us; a spirit of love, goodness, and mercy. This is what makes Christmas a time of goodwill and peace.

Are You Willing?

Finally, the reaction we can have to the announcement, "You're going to have a baby," is to accept it with joy. The interview with Gabriel ended when Mary said, "Here am I, the servant of the Lord; let it be with me according to your word." She accepted the fact of motherhood gladly. To be the mother of Jesus was an honor to her, because she felt totally unworthy of the high calling. She refers to herself as a "servant" which means a "bond-servant" or "slave." As a servant of God, she lived to serve and please God. That's why she could say "yes" to motherhood with joy. Indeed, she had other reasons to be glad. She was informed that she had found favor with God. God picked her out of all the other young women in the nation and found her worthy of being the mother of God's Son. Every woman dreamed of some day being the mother of the Messiah. She was the chosen one. She was to be the means by which God would save the people. In the future countless people would honor her as the mother of God.

If God was to send God's Son on earth, God had to have the acceptance and cooperation of Mary. She cheerfully and obediently submitted to God's will. Her body was to be God's instrument by which God would enter the world as a human being. God depends upon human willingness and cooperation to perform God's divine will on earth. So, if Christ is to be born in us, we must let God use us. Like Mary, we need to offer our bodies as God's instruments in carrying out the will of the Lord. This calls for submission and dedication. A person, to be God's agent in the world, must be committed and consecrated. It calls for a surrendered life. Mary shows us that you can be a "nobody" and still be mightily used by God. Dwight L. Moody once said, "The world is still waiting to see what God can do with one totally surrendered life." Grenfell heard him say that and he decided to let God do something with his life. Look what God did with one surrendered peasant girl's life about 2,000 years ago. Something good can happen to you when you turn over your life to God's service. God can do miracles with a life totally dedicated to the Lord.

You know, Christmas deals with the birth of Jesus long ago in a manger. But the truth is that for you Christ was never born unless he is born in you. There is no true Christmas without Christ's being born in you. Maybe he has been born in you, but in that case every Christmas is a time of re-birth. Each year Gabriel comes to you as he came to the Virgin Mary with the announcement, "You're going to have a baby!" Christ is waiting, wanting, longing to be born in you this Christmas. But he will not be born unless you want him in you, unless you agree. Will there be a place in the inn of your heart for him? If you are willing to have the baby Jesus born in you, pray the words of Phillips Brooks:

O Holy Child of Bethlehem,
Descend to us, we pray;
Cast out our sin, and enter in,
Be born in us today.

God With A Human Face

In the beginning was the Word, and the Word was with God, and the Word was God. He was in the beginning with God. All things came into being through him, and without him not one thing came into being. What has come into being in him was life, and the life was the light of all people. The light shines in the darkness, and the darkness did not overcome it.

There was a man sent from God, whose name was John. He came as a witness to testify to the light, so that all might believe through him. He himself was not the light, but he came to testify to the light. The true light, which enlightens everyone, was coming into the world.

He was in the world, and the world came into being through him; yet the world did not know him. He came to what was his own, and his own people did not accept him. But to all who received him, who believed in his name, he gave power to become children of God, who were born, not of blood or of the will of the flesh or of the will of man, but of God.

And the word became flesh and lived among us, and we have seen his glory, the glory as of a father's only son, full of grace and truth. (John testified to him and cried out, "This was he of whom I said, 'He who comes after me ranks ahead of me because he was before me.' ") From his fullness we have all received, grace upon grace. The law indeed was given through Moses; grace and truth came through Jesus Christ. No one has ever seen God. It is God the only Son, who is close to the Father's heart, who has made him known.

— John 1:1-18

After only a week of married life, a young husband had to leave his bride to fight in the war. Though they were a half-world apart in distance, they frequently exchanged letters and occasionally he would send her a gift to remind her of his love. Then one night there was a sudden and unexpected knock on her door. Cautiously she opened it and to her amazement there stood her soldier-husband. On his face was a grin that extended from ear to ear. They ran into each other's arms and laughed and cried with the joy of reunion.

In times past God has been sending words and gifts of love to his children. In various ways through priests and prophets God has been sending messages of love and truth. Continually God has been sending gifts to us. But, on Christmas night God knocks on the door of humankind and presents himself as a man, a God with a human face. As John says in our text, no man has ever seen God until now we see him in the face of the Babe of Bethlehem. God becomes a man, identifies himself with man that we might know God personally, physically, realistically. This is what humans need today. We are constantly asking, "Where is God?" "What is God like?" and "Where can I find God?" Those questions are answered in God's becoming a human being. To look at Jesus is to see God. Look into the face of Christ and you look into the true nature of God. In the text John says, "We have seen his glory ..." In Jesus' face we see the glory of God.

A Face Of Life

On this Christmas day the Christ child is the center of attention. All eyes are upon the baby Jesus. When we look into the face of this child, what do we see? Our text tells us that one thing we see is that God is life. "In him was life," says verse 4. Life was in Christ, and automatically we understand that God is life. Another name for God is Life with a capital "L." God's very essence is life. God is Being as over against Non-being. It is not a case of God's having life but that God is life. Jesus once said, "I am the way, the truth, and the life." As life, God is the author of all life. Our text refers to God as the creator of all things: "All things were made through him ..." This life of God's as seen in Christ is permanent.

40

It is not a matter of threescore years and ten and that is the end. God's life is eternal, from everlasting to everlasting. That is why eternal life, which we Christians claim, is a gift, never a human attainment. The life God gives is God's own life, and as God is eternal, the life God gives is eternal.

Because of this, Christians have life in the very midst of physical death. When Norman Vincent Peale was a young minister in Brooklyn he saw one Christmas Eve two Christmas wreaths on a door. The one had a red ribbon and the other had a black ribbon. He sensed that the family had a death. Although he was not their pastor, he felt constrained to go and offer his sympathy. It was a family with children who had just moved there recently. When Peale knocked on the door, the man said, "Come in." In the living room was a casket holding the body of a six-year-old girl. When Peale offered his condolence, the father replied. "It's all right. She is with the Lord, you know." At the same time the mother was upstairs reading the Bible before two younger brothers went to bed. He heard her read, "Because I live, you shall live also."

Real, genuine, and true life for a person is life in God. To have life, a person must have Christ in him by faith and Christ must be born in him. According to the Bible, death is not only physical death but it is separation from God. The farther we get away from God the less life we have. If we have no faith, if we reject Christ, we live only an earthly existence which is banal, meaningless, and frustrating. This means that life is a relationship with God in Christ. Do you ask, "How does one maintain a relationship with the Author of Life?" To keep in touch with God means that we must pray daily, continuously. Worship is a way to keep close to God. Taking time out each day in private devotions when you read the Bible, reflect, and meditate is necessary to keep in contact with God. Jesus once said, "I am the vine, you are the branches." When a branch is broken off the vine, you know what happens. It withers and dies. To have true life, each of us must maintain constant contact with God, living in God's presence at all times. This is one main reason for God's coming to earth in the form of man. God came in Jesus to die for humans. He was born to die that all might have life. It meant the cross, because through the cross a sacrifice for sin would be made. Sin is what separates from God, and separation from God means death. Christ came to redeem us, to save us from death. By putting us at one with God, by restoring fellowship with God, we have life. So, when we look into the face of Jesus, we see that God is life.

A Face Of Light

Take a second look into the face of this helpless child in the manger and what do you see? According to our text, we can see that God is light. "In him was life, and the life was the light of all people . . . The true light which enlightens everyone was coming into the world." There is a radiance in the face of Jesus. It reflects the shining face of God, a face brighter than the sun. It is really too bright to look at and thus we dare look only into the face of Jesus which reflects the light.

Of course, we do not know the exact calendar day when Jesus was born. But, was it not significant that the church chose December 25 as his birthday? It comes at the darkest time of the year, because December 21 is considered the shortest day of the year. Our world has been described as a people sitting in darkness. Because of this the world needs light, and God knew it! That is why Christ came: to lighten our darkness.

Do you need any proof that we are in darkness? There is the darkness of crime, sin, and disobedience. The FBI reports that 75 percent of all crimes take place in the dark. Crime flourishes in poorly lighted areas. That is one reason for street lights — watch out for those dark alleys! Businessmen keep their stores and plants lighted at night to discourage break-ins. When you leave home for a vacation, you arrange to have lights burn during the night to make thieves think you are home. Also, there is the darkness of hatred. "Hate, Inc." sponsors an annual "National Hate Week" in America to foster unbridled hatred. Think of the hatred between Catholics and Protestants in Ireland. The darkness of hatred is overwhelming in the Middle East where Jew and Arab hate each other to the threat of another world war. This hatred was expressed when three Arab guerillas crossed the border and killed four Jews. This so aroused hatred that the Jews killed the guerillas and threw their bodies out of an upper story window. They doused the bodies with gasoline, set them afire, and chanted, "Kill them again! Kill them again!" Think also of the darkness of our ignorance in spite of all our books, schools, and learned societies. We are in the dark when it comes to some of our main problems. Our leaders frankly admit they do not have the answer to problems such as cancer, inflation, the energy crisis, and even something as simple as the common cold. It is said that the only known cure for a cold is to come home, put your hat on the bedpost, and drink liquor until you see two hats. Then go to bed and sleep it off!

As Goethe was dying, he cried out, "Light, more light!" That is the cry of our dark world this Christmas. Jesus is the light, for he said, "I am the light of the world." He is the light because he is of the Father and is a reflection of the God of light. When this baby in the manger grew up, he told his followers, "You are in the light of the world." At once this points to the great need for Christ and the church in the world. In Christ and his body, the church is the source of the world's light. To have Christ and the church is not something you can take or leave. It is a basic essential of life and of a good society. Light is needed to show men the truth, to point out the path that leads to life and peace. Light is needed to dispel the darkness of wickedness and crime in the world that it may become a safe place in which to live.

If we see that God is light in the face of Jesus, how does this light come to the world? It comes in Christ. Don't you see the radiance surrounding the manger? Since Christ is no longer in the world, the light of God comes through Christ's people, the church. Jesus said that we, his disciples, are the light of the world. If there are over 100 million Christians in America, why is there so much darkness here? If there are

43

about a billion Christians in the world, why is there so much dark hatred in the world? Could it be that we Christians are failing to be lights to the world?

Is it possible that we have allowed the light to go out in our lamps? Are we like the foolish virgins in the parable? There was once a train and school bus collision. Seven children were killed. Later there was an investigation held. The signal man at the crossing was severely cross-examined. He insisted that he was swinging his lantern vigorously. The next day a friend complimented him for standing up under the heavy fire of questioning and sticking to his story. He replied, "I was afraid that the lawyer was going to ask me whether the lantern was lit!" This seems to be so much like the church today. We have equipment, buildings, programs, and procedures. We go through the mechanics of our religion. But often the light of Christ is not in our church business. People in the darkness cannot see the Light. This light of Christ needs to be rekindled at this Christmas time as Christ once more comes to be born anew, to burn again in our lives and churches.

If the light has gone out of the church, it may be due to the fact that in each of us the light of Christ no longer burns. When a little girl got home from church one Sunday where she had heard a sermon on "Let your light shine," she asked her mother what that meant. The mother explained that the light shone when we were sweet, kind and good. The next Sunday in the nursery, the child caused an uproar to the extent that the teacher had to get her mother to quiet her down. Remembering what she was told the previous Sunday the little girl blurted out, "I have blowed myself out!" Maybe that has happened to us also. We have blown out the light of Christ and are living in sin. If that is the case, we need to take Christ the Light once again into our hearts. Take the candle of your heart to Christ the Light and let him reignite your candle by touching him. If each of us is a candle in a dark world, the world will be brighter because we let our little lights shine and God will be glorified by our good works.

A Face Of Love

When we look at the God with the human face, we see love. There is nothing but kindness, tenderness and understanding in that face of Jesus. And this is the way it is with God. In a letter John simply says, "God is love." In our text we are told that "from his fullness we have all received, grace upon grace." In this same text, we see God's love in that by faith in Christ we become children of God. Luther considered John 3:16 the greatest text in the Bible: "God so loved the world that he gave his only Son ..." It is like Hallmark advertises, "When you care enough to send the very best." God cared enough for humankind to send God's very best. The very best was God *in* Jesus. Christmas, then, is a festival of love because we are now convinced as we gaze into the face of Jesus that God truly loves each of us.

How can we be sure that God loves each of us? Love is best expressed in giving to the one loved. That is why at Christmas we have this mad craze of shopping for gifts. It all began with God's giving to humans and their giving to Jesus as the Wise Men brought their gifts to the manger-child. Gifts express love. They are physical tokens of love. We say, "I love you," with a gift. Of course, there is a danger in this. It is quite possible that this principle can be prostituted so the meaning is distorted and nullified. We all know that gifts can be given out of a sense of duty and obligation. Though we may not want to give, we are ashamed not to have a gift for one whom we know will be giving to us. Often a gift is presented without any love at all. We will all agree that such a gift without the heart of the giver is bare indeed and it may just as well not be given.

So, it is not the material gift that is really the final proof of love. It is the person in the gift. Even better is to give yourself as a gift. This is what God did for us. God emptied himself of God's godly powers and prestige and humbled himself to be born of a virgin, and God came to the people of God who did not receive him. As Paul said, "God was in Christ."

In Jesus God gave himself to the world. And the tragedy of every Christmas is "He came to his own home, and his own people received him not." As God gave himself in Jesus, Christ gave himself to humankind. He came to die for humans. When he hung on a cross, Jesus did not die for himself or for his sins. He died for our sins. He gave his all that we might have life and light. As Jesus said, "Greater love has no man than this that he lay down his life for his friends. You are my friends . . ."

It is too late to take up the question of what gift would be the best you could give this Christmas. But, we do not have to wait until next Christmas to give this gift. The very best gift you could give is yourself, just as God and Jesus gave themselves to us. A lawyer once said that the greatest gift he ever got was one Christmas when his dad gave him a little box. Inside was a note: "Son, this year I will give you 365 hours, an hour after dinner each day in the coming year. We will talk about what you want to talk about, go where you want to go, play what you want to play. It will be your hour." The attorney said that his father kept the promise, and then renewed the gift each year. He confessed, "It was the greatest gift I ever had in my life."

Every one of us would appreciate a gift like that. And so would God! In our liturgy we have the offering when we give to God our material gifts as an expression of our love and faith in God. But, there is another form of offering called the "offertory." It is the time when we re-give ourselves to God and his Christ. We give ourselves as we sing "Create in me a clean heart, O God . . ." This is a far more expensive and appreciated gift than the check for $1,000 we may have put on the offering plate. On the mission field an old lady walked two miles to church in bare feet because she was too poor to buy shoes. When the offering came, she had not a cent to give but she walked up with the ushers, kissed the pastor, and told him that she would like to give herself to God in place of money. This Christmas God has given the supreme gift of himself in Jesus. Now is the time for us to respond with our chief gift to God — the giving of ourselves in allegiance, love and service.

When you see God in the face of Jesus, a miracle happens. People see God in your face. When Jacob met Esau after years of estrangement, he was met with love and forgiveness. It made Jacob say to Esau, "For truly to see your face is like seeing the face of God, with such favor have you received me." When Stephen was dying from being stoned to death for his Christian witness, the Book of Acts says, "His face was like the face of an angel." Because at Christmas we were given a God with a human face, we humans can have the face of God!

Wrinkled
Wrappings

Now there was a man in Jerusalem whose name was Simeon; this man was righteous and devout, looking forward to the consolation of Israel, and the Holy Spirit rested on him. It had been revealed to him by the Holy Spirit that he would not see death before he had seen the Lord's Messiah. Guided by the Spirit, Simeon came into the temple; and when the parents brought in the child Jesus, to do for him what was customary under the law, Simeon took him in his arms and praised God, saying, "Master, now you are dismissing your servant in peace, according to your word; for my eyes have seen your salvation, which you have prepared in the presence of all peoples, a light for revelation to the Gentiles and for glory to your people Israel."

And the child's father and mother were amazed at what was being said about him. Then Simeon blessed them and said to his mother Mary, "This child is destined for the falling and the rising of many in Israel, and to be a sign that will be opposed so that the inner thoughts of many will be revealed — and a sword will pierce your own soul too."

There was also a prophet, Anna the daughter of Phanuel, of the tribe of Asher. She was of a great age, having lived with her husband seven years after her marriage, then as a widow to the age of eighty-four. She never left the temple but worshiped there with fasting and prayer night and day. At that moment she came, and began to praise God and to speak about the child to all who were looking for the redemption of Jerusalem.

— Luke 2:25-38

On the Sunday after Christmas we were asked to come to a church to preach. The pastor of the church asked us to come early and have dinner with his family. We said we would but

49

we urged him and his wife not to go to any trouble with the dinner. He replied, "We will not be having much, just some Christmas leftovers." On the first Sunday after Christmas that is just about the way it is in various ways. Church attendance today compared with the Christmas Eve service looks like "leftovers." Christmas leftovers come in the form of bills for gifts bought for Christmas. Decorations left over from Christmas, boxes and wrapping paper need to be thrown away.

In our gospel lesson it appears as though we have leftover people, Simeon and Anna. They are aged: one is ready to die and the widow is 84 years old. They are leftovers from the meal of life. By their wrinkled, shriveled bodies they appear as wrinkled wrappings. But, leftovers can be good and delicious as the main meal. This was the case with the couple in wrinkled wrappings. They saw something 40 days after Christmas that nobody up to that time had seen. The shepherds were stunned at the sight of the angels and all they did was to go and see the sight at the manger. The Wise Men saw in the manger-child only a new king. Herod and other high government officials were afraid of losing their positions because they heard a new king was born. Religious leaders, scribes, and rabbis knew where the Messiah was to be born but they did not bother to go and see whether he came. The only ones who recognized the Messiah in the man-child, God in Jesus, were two aged people.

And we seem to have the same problem. Do we recognize a good thing when we see it? Do we see God in Jesus today? There are two billion people in today's world who do not see God in Jesus, for they are non-Christians. Most of the Jews in the world are still praying for Messiah to come, because they do not see Jesus as the Messiah.

In our text God asks us, "What do you see in Jesus?" We wonder how Simeon and Anna could have such insight into the nature of Jesus. In our day we do not usually have a high opinion of old folks. After age 40 wrinkles come. You begin to lose hair and some teeth. Eyesight dims and glasses become necessary. Hearing gets more difficult. Fat accumulates in your midsection. Muscles shrink and joints stiffen. The heart gets less efficient and the flow of hormones declines. It is claimed that after age 45, you lose 100,000 brain cells per day. How could people in this kind of physical condition have such insight? In spite of their physical ailments and limitations, these two old people had an insight into Jesus that many do not have. Apparently, they had a fabulous new way of seeing. They can teach us how to get insight into Christ.

Good People

If we study aged Simeon and Anna, we see what it takes to find God in Jesus, the fulfillment of the promise of the Messiah-Savior. There was the quality of goodness. The text says they were "righteous." It is a fact that sin keeps us from seeing God. Sin makes us dirty and we can not see very well through dirty glasses. Sin causes darkness — the darkness of doubt, despair and selfishness. Because of our sins this Christmas, we have not been able to see anything more in the manger than a human baby. In the city of Atlanta alone, shoplifters one Christmas season stole more than a half million dollars' worth of merchandise, half taken by employees. Some have been so busy with personal and business affairs that they did not have room for Christ to come into their hearts. Jesus taught that the pure in heart see God. Doctors say that this is literally true: a dirty heart can cause poor vision. There is a disease that causes ulcers to form on the inner walls of the heart. This condition affects the blood vessels of the eyes which become bloodshot. If the heart condition is not cured, the blood vessels in the eyes burst and the person becomes blind. "Who shall ascend unto the hill of the Lord? He who has clean hands and a pure heart ..." A good man is a godly man who knows and sees God.

Devout People

Simeon and Anna were able to see God in Christ when Mary and Joseph brought him in the temple when he was only 40 days old, because of their devotion to God. Our text describes the aged ones as "devout." Both of them were in God's House, the temple. Where can you find a better place to see God? They fasted daily, not once a year as in Lent or once a week. Through fasting they disciplined themselves that they might have a closer relationship with the heavenly Father. They were people of prayer, praying night and day. Prayer is being in touch with God, being aware of his constant presence, and reflecting upon God's will and nature. Prayer is more than a sentence prayer before meals or an "Our Father" at bedtime. Prayer is fellowship with God, with or without words.

All of this is necessary to see God in a person like Jesus. Saint Paul said that only the spiritual can discern spiritual matters. The secularist, the atheist, and the agnostic have no sensitivity to God and related spiritual concerns. Every bush is aflame with God and they stand around picking blackberries! This explains why many do not see God in Jesus. They do not know God. One day the great novelist, Mark Twain, was telling about all the famous people he knew. His little daughter stunned him when she said, "Daddy, you know almost everybody except God, don't you?" And that is about the way it is with many of us. No wonder we cannot see the Messiah in Jesus.

Inspired People

Granted, we are not talking about anything easy. After all, this baby was only 40 days old, and all babies look very much alike. Is it expecting too much to think an average passerby could hail Jesus as the Messiah while being carried in his mother's arms to the temple? Yet, this is the uncanny insight aged Simeon and Anna, wrinkled wrappings, had one day in the temple. How could they do it? What did they have that we don't have? Another characteristic of this couple was the possession of the Holy Spirit. The Spirit led Simeon to the temple, told him he would see the Christ before he died, and opened his eyes to see the Christ in the baby. Here is the ultimate key to spiritual insight. The Spirit enlightens us, and Jesus said that the Spirit would guide us into all truth. When Stephen was being stoned to death, he cried out that he saw the Son of God standing at the right hand of the Father. This vision came as a result of the spirit's possession of him.

For many the Spirit is a mysterious factor. We are not sure we have the Spirit, and if we do not have him, we are not sure how to get him. The Spirit is the third person of the Trinity; he is God, for God is Spirit. He comes to us through the Word of God and the Sacraments. The Spirit comes to us when we receive baptism and Holy Communion and when we hear or read the Scriptures. The Spirit gives us vision and enables us to dream dreams. If we want to receive the Spirit or grow in the Spirit, it is obvious that we need to faithfully come to church for the Word and Sacraments.

Just as we ought to see God in the Baby Jesus, we should see good in our fellowman. Take a baby. Do you see the good that child may someday do? Can you see the potential? Is a human being worth only the value of the chemicals in his body now estimated to be about $17. Pity a child whose mother says to him, "You are no good, you were a mistake and I never should have borne you. You will spend your years behind bars." Though man is sinful and unclean, we need to see gold in garbage and treasure in trash. In 1844 Tischendorf found in St. Catherine's monastery 129 leaves of an ancient manuscript of the Bible in a trash can ready to be burned. Americans throw away millions of tons of garbage a year, but now cities are finding they can turn garbage into profits. Out of every ton of garbage experts expects to get 1 barrel of oil. When we see good in people, we encourage them to be what we think them to be. In the musical, *The Man Of La Mancha,* Aldonza is a common prostitute working in a cheap inn. When Don Quixote sees her, he calls her Dulcinea and sees her as a lovely, beautiful maiden. At first she laughs at him and shouts, "My name is not Dulcinea. I am Aldonza, Aldonza the whore!" By the time of the final scene when Don

Quixote is dying, she becomes Dulcinea through the confidence of a man who seems insane. Look at your child and see someone great and someday he may be just that! Look at your friends as people of character and promise and they will usually fulfill your high expectations.

Now, in the second place, God asks us, "What are you going to do about what you see?" If you see Jesus as God in human flesh, if you now perceive that Jesus truly is the promised Messiah and Savior of the world, what are you going to do about it? When the famous missionary, William Carey, was home on furlough, he was given a standing ovation. Then they went on to the next speaker, but before the next man could begin his address, Carey leaped to the center of the stage and cried, "Aren't you going to do anything about it? Aren't you going to do anything about it?" To see God in the baby Jesus is an earth-shattering event, a once-in-a-lifetime vision. You just have to do something about it. The vision will not let you go home and take up religion-as-usual.

Simeon and Anna in our text show us what we can do about this Messiah-Christ born not many days ago. The couple in wrinkled wrappings responded to the Christ-child with worship. This is the spirit of Christmas: "Come and worship, come and worship Christ the new-born king." In a spirit of worship Simeon and Anna thanked and praised God for the sending of the Messiah. Simeon broke out in song which the church calls the Nunc Dimittis: "Lord, now lettest thou thy servant depart in peace . . ." His song is still used in our worship services: in the Holy Communion and Vesper services.

Apparently even many Christians do not see Christ in Jesus because they do not react with worship. According to a Gallup poll, about 40 percent of church members go to church in America. This means 60 percent of our nominal Christians are not glad when it is said, "Let us go into the house of the Lord . . ." Those who see God in Christ respond with a free and spontaneous worship of praise and thanks. Heartily we sing, "Beautiful Savior, King of creation" or in adoration we sing, "Jesus, my Lord, my God, my all." If Jesus is the

Son of God, if Jesus is the Savior and Lord, then we must fall down before him in adoration and praise.

Self For Christ

Another reaction to seeing God in Jesus is dedication of self to Christ. Simeon and Anna accepted Jesus as the Messiah. Anna witnessed to that fact to those around her in the temple. Simeon took the child from Mary and with the baby in his arms he sang praise to God. He said, "Master, now you are dismissing your servant in peace, for my eyes have seen your salvation . . ." He is saying that now he has seen everything. He is ready and content to die. His life is now fulfilled. Since the Messiah came, he can die in peace and in hope of eternal life. He surrendered all, even his life.

This is the way people have always felt when they came to see God in Jesus. They have found the pearl of great price, and they sell all they have to buy that one pearl. He is the very best and they are willing to pay the price to get it. Jesus is worth everything, even your very life. This is the way it was with the Disciples who after meeting Jesus left all and followed him. Saint Paul says that all his previous possessions were as refuse compared to the excellence of knowing Christ. When Saint Francis of Assisi became a Christian, he took off all his clothes before his father and bishop and embarrassed both of them. Francis wanted nothing of the past, for now he was going into a new life of service in Christ. To see who Jesus really is makes one fall down before him and give him complete and absolute allegiance till death. Richard Watson Gilder put it this way and may he speak for each of us:

If Jesus Christ is a man —
And only a man, — I say
That of all mankind I cleave to him,
And to him will I cleave alway.

If Jesus Christ is a God —
  And the only God, — swear
I will follow him through heaven and hell,
  The earth, the sea, and the air!

In His Service

This devotion to Jesus as Son of God is expressed also, in service. This was true with Simeon and Anna. They served in the temple. Anna served by witnessing to Jesus as the Christ. In our text we are told that Simeon blessed God and blessed the Holy Family. One who has found God in Christ wants to be Christ's slave or servant for life. To serve him is a privilege and honor. Our highest pleasure is to do something for Christ and His kingdom on earth. We delight in his cause. We love to be in his presence. This is now our reason for living. This is what life is all about. We are here to advance the Kingdom, to serve the King. From the time I was a youth, these words of Tennyson captured my imagination:

Man am I grown, a man's work must I do,
Follow the deer? Follow the Christ, the king,
Live pure, speak true, right wrong, follow the
  king —
Else, wherefore born?

Granted, this is quite a contrast to what you find in some churches. The complaint is heard, "Nobody wants to do anything. People won't visit prospects. Vacancies are on the church school staff. The choir loft is half-full." This indicates that some church people have not yet seen the Christ in the Baby Jesus. They see only another human being, a tiny helpless baby. Christmas is just another holiday. If God is in Jesus and he is really and truly the Savior-Lord and King, then I must serve him gladly and willingly. To serve Christ is humankind's highest distinction. In the church and out of the church, in the home and out in the world, be Christ's happy servant. In that there is life and happiness.

56

A man and his grandson were walking on the beach when they met an old minister friend who was disgruntled. Nothing was any good to him. He complained he was suffering from a sunstroke. The lad listened to the conversation, and when they continued their walk, the boy said, "Granddad, I hope that you never suffer from a sunset." To be able to recognize a good thing when it comes, you do not have to suffer from a sunset and be like aged Simeon and Anna in wrinkled wrappings. If you have the spiritual qualities of these old saints, you will be able to see in Jesus the Christ, your Lord and Savior. Seeing the Son in Jesus will make your life a continual sunrise and your life will be filled with sunshine.

You Are
A Name!

*After eight days had passed, it was time to circumcise
the child; and he was called Jesus, the name given by the
angel before he was conceived in the womb.*
— Luke 2:21

Today a name does not seem to mean much. We glibly ask,
"What is a name?" As children we chanted, "Sticks and stones
can break my bones, but names can never hurt me." A person's name is only a label, a mark of identification. A name
answers the question, "Who are you?" Because a name seems
to mean little in our time, some give their children odd names.
One had the name "Miss Ima Hogg." One mother named her
daughter "Alpha Omega" because she was her first and hope-
fully her last child. A black child was named "Nevaseena"
because her father died before her birth and he had never seen
her. No wonder 50,000 people go to courts annually to have
their names changed.

In the Bible it is the opposite. A name is most important,
as important as the person named. In biblical thinking you
do not have a name; you are a name. That is why God chose
the name of his Son. Gabriel told Mary that she should name
her child "Jesus." On this first day of a new year the church
celebrates the naming of Jesus when he was eight days old,
the time of his circumcision. In the church the greatest and
most popular name is Jesus. On crosses and paraments and
in windows you see IHS, the first three letters of the Greek
word for Jesus. A professor studied the names in *Reader's
Digest* for 20 years and found Jesus the name most often used.
Why is this so? Why is Jesus' name so important that we set
aside this day to honor it? What does the name mean to us
today as Christians? Because of Jesus, a Christian does not

only have a name but is a name. A name for a Christian is not only for identification but for the purpose of identity.

What You Are

First of all, your name defines your nature. It does not only say who you are but what you are. In the Bible one's name is the same as his nature, character and the sum total of his personality. Your name is you, your very being, what makes you. Because of this a man's name and nature are one. Despise a name and you despise a person with the name. Exalt a name and you honor the person.

This is the case with the name of God and Jesus. Humans have always had the problem of learning God's name. Since humans cannot fully know God, God's name cannot be known. When God called Moses to go back to Egypt to deliver the captives, Moses asked, "What shall I say when they ask me, What is his name?" God replied, "I am who I am." The Hebrew Bible does not have the vowels in the name of God to prevent man from pronouncing or misusing it: YHWH. They used a substitute name "Adonai" which is translated "Lord." The name of God was never to be spoken because it was synonymous with the nature of God.

Because of this relationship of name and nature, we can understand the holiness of God's name. God is holy and thus God's name is holy. To misuse God's name is a grievous sin, for an irreverent use of the name desecrates God and is blasphemy. To misuse and abuse the name is to violate the holy nature of God. This was so important that God gave Moses as one of the Ten Commandments, "Thou shalt not take the name of the Lord thy God in vain ..." In our profane culture, we seem to have forgotten this commandment. In daily conversation, in literature, and on the stage we hear God's name taken in vain at a rate of almost every other sentence. In the days of Watergate the nation was stunned and shocked when they read the transcripts of President Nixon with repeated blanks and the explanation, "Expletive Deleted." A Christian will have no part of this and will refrain from any use of God's name except for prayer and worship. God's name is to be used with a sense of awe and respect and with a holy reverence.

Because the name and nature are one, we can understand, too, the power of God's name. If the name is the same as God's nature, we know that God is all-powerful. As a God of omnipotence, there is nothing too hard for God, not even the impossible. Knowing this, we pray in Jesus' name. Here is the power of prayer, not in the words or act of praying but in the fact that the prayer is made in Jesus' name. Because of Jesus, God hears and answers our prayers. If our prayers are according to God's will, God has the power to answer our prayers.

The power of Jesus' name is demonstrated in healing. Christians have always brought healing to people, just as Jesus did when he was on earth. When Peter and John saw a cripple at the Beautiful Gate, they healed him by saying, "In the name of Jesus, rise up and walk." The healing done today by Christians is not done by any personal magnetism or special knowledge, but it is made possible by the very power of Jesus' name.

In our time we are concerned about exorcising the devil in people. The need for getting the devil out of devil-possessed people was brought to people's attention by the classic movie *The Exorcist*. In that picture all the doctors and all the psychiatrists and all the pills and drugs could not drive the devil out of the 12-year-old child. Priests were called in to help her. The devil was finally driven out by the holy name of Jesus. This is because the name of Jesus is identical with the nature of Jesus. This nature is good and holy, and the devil cannot tolerate such holiness. He flees when Christ comes.

A Change Of Name

What is the case with God's name is also true with a person's name. Your name gives you your character, not only who but what you are. It is not your family name but your given name that describes your nature. When a person's name is too

61

far from a person's personality, we usually give the person a nickname. For years a prominent Georgia politician was known as "Sloppy" Floyd. Apparently the Apostles were not satisfied with the name "Joseph," for they named him "Barnabas," meaning "Son of Encouragement." When a person's nature changes, his name is changed. After Abram's call, he was known as Abraham. Jesus changed the name of Simon to Peter meaning "rock." After his conversion Saul was called Paul. Harry Golden, editor of the *Carolina Israelite* and writer of the best seller, *Out Of Africa*, served a term in federal prison for mail fraud. When he was released, he decided to live a new life, moved south and changed his name.

You might be asking at this time, "What kind of a name do I have? Does it honestly and properly reflect my nature?" Well, maybe your given name of Tom or Mary may not say much about you. But, you have a Christian name which does describe your true nature as a person. You have a Christian name given at your baptism when you received a new nature by the Holy Spirit. This is similar to Jesus' circumcision, a rite that established a covenant with God resulting in the child being made a member of God's people. In like manner, we are born again at baptism when God makes us new creatures in Christ. When we were baptized a pastor spoke our name and said, "I baptize you in the Name of the Father and of the Son and of the Holy Spirit." You were baptized in the name of Jesus. You now have his nature, his mind, spirit and attitude. Now you are a Christian and you bear the name of Christ. For this reason baptism is sometimes called "Christening"; it is the time when a person is made a Christian by God's gracious act of adoption. Legally we get our name when the birth certificate is sent to our parents, but spiritually we get our name when we are "Christened." This is necessary because we come into the world not as sons of God by nature. Paul teaches that we become children of God only through adoption, and the act of adoption is baptism.

Having a Christian name which denotes a Christian nature, we face a daily challenge to live up to our names. We are to act according to what we are. The Christian life is a process of becoming what we are, bearers of the name of Christ. As a son went off to college, his father said, "Son, remember who you are." When a child, Queen Victoria was told, "Be loyal to the royal in you." Christian, you are somebody because you are Somebody's. You have a Christian name; you are a name, a Christian.

What You Are To Do

In the second place, a name describes a person's work. It shows what he is to do with his life. It explains the purpose, mission and ideals for life. The name describes a person's destiny, God's plan for his life, what he is here for.

Jesus' name reveals not only his nature but his work. The name, Jesus, means "Yahweh saves," or "He shall save." This tells us just about all we need to know about Jesus. If he came to save, then he was the Messiah, the Son of God, deliverer and redeemer. Jesus came, as you have heard many times before, to die for our sins. His mission was to reconcile people to God that they might be in harmony with each other. This meant that sin had to be dealt with, for sin means opposition and rebellion to God. Jesus was born to die, and for this reason the cradle and the cross are two sides of the coin of Jesus' life. We cannot help but thank and praise God for Jesus' coming because his mission was to liberate people from their bondage to themselves and their sins. Christ came to bless, to offer mercy and peace to all humankind. His name reveals that his purpose in coming was to bless, to help everyone, to give life to the dying, and light to those in darkness. No wonder we sing, "All hail the power of Jesus' name." "His name is wonderful," a gospel song says.

Every Christian can now say that "my goal in life is to do with my life the same as Jesus did with his life." You and I have Christian names received at baptism. Now we have the identical purpose and goal in life.

As Christians we witness to Jesus' name as the means of getting right with God. We call it "salvation" or "being saved." In the first chapter of his gospel, John says, "But to all who received him, who believed in his name, he gave power to become children of God." The Bible promises "Every one who calls upon the name of the Lord will be saved." Following in the steps of Jesus, bearing his name, Christians are concerned about "saving souls," that is, bringing people to the life and love of God in Christ. How do we go about it? We, like Philip and Andrew when the Greeks came saying, "Sir, we would see Jesus," take people to Jesus. We serve as midwives who help people to be born again as they believe in the Name of Jesus. This may sound too simple and too easy to get right with God, but it nevertheless is true. Life and peace with God come when you put your trust in the Name of Jesus. As Christians it is our privilege to proclaim the name of Jesus that people might be saved.

We also serve in Jesus' name. His name indicated that he was to save his people. He saved them by serving them. With a Christian name that is our purpose in life, too. This answers the question we often ask, "Why should I help people?" There are many reasons, some good and some not so good. But, the best reason for helping people in need is to do it in Jesus' name. That means that we love people for Jesus' sake. We see Jesus in our neighbor, and what we do for him, we do for Jesus. This is the basic and noblest motive for Christian service. If we do it only for humanitarian reasons, we will eventually grow weary in well-doing. That is what happened to the social action program and the civil rights efforts of recent years. We ran out of steam and the train of human progress has slowed to a halt. We do not help people because they are worthy of help or because they are lovable. We help them in the name of Jesus. The Master said, "Whoever gives a little one a cup of water in my name, he shall not lose his reward." A father and son were walking down a busy street on Christmas Eve. An unshaven dirty old beggar clutched the arm of the father and begged for money. The boy backed away in repulsiveness.

The father said, "Son, this is Christmas Eve. You shouldn't treat a man like that!" The boy replied, "Dad, he's nothing but a bum." The father answered, "He may not have made much out of himself but he's still a child of God." Taking a dollar out of his pocket, he continued, "Give this to the man and tell him you are giving it in Christ's name." Reluctantly, the boy went after the beggar and said, "Excuse me, sir, I give you this money in the name of Christ." In utter amazement, the beggar took off his hat, and bowed graciously, and said, "And I thank you, young sir, in the name of Christ."

If we bear the name of Christian, we will live daily in Jesus' name. In all of our actions, in the daily chores at home, work or school, we will do everything in Jesus' name. This means we will do all in the mind and spirit of Jesus — honestly and cheerfully. Paul urges us to do this: "And whatever you do, in word or deed, do everything in the name of the Lord Jesus ..."

A woman went into the office of a cemetery manager and complained, "I can't find my husband's grave. I know he's buried here." The manager asked, "What is the name?" "Thomas Jackson," she replied. Looking through his card index, the manager said, "We have no Thomas Jackson but we do have an Elizabeth Jackson." "That's him," she affirmed. "Everything's in my name." We, too, can say everything is in God's name, for this is God's universe and we are the children of God. Likewise, we Christians do everything in Jesus' name. We praise his name; we pray in his name; we heal in his name. To be saved we believe in his name. And some day, God willing, we shall die in his name. Until then we live to make his name glorious.

Happy
Next Year?

*I will greatly rejoice in the Lord, my whole being shall
exult in my God; for he has clothed me with the garments
of salvation, he has covered me with the robe of righteousness, as a bridegroom decks himself with a garland,
and as a bride adorns herself with her jewels. For as the
earth brings forth its shoots, and as a garden causes what
is sown in it to spring up, so the Lord God will cause
righteousness and praise to spring up before all the nations.* — Isaiah 61:10-11

At the beginning of a new year it is customary for us to
greet each other with "Happy New Year!" Do we mean "day"
rather than "year"? We give the greeting on New Year's Day,
but on this seventh day of the new year, are we still saying
it? Are we wishing friends to be happy for only a day or for
a whole year? How can one be happy for a whole year when
the forecast for the new year may predict unhappy times? Can
you be happy if in the coming year you may have less to eat,
if you must make old clothes do for another year, if a vacation is out of the question, and if you must worry about the
bills coming due?

Regardless of conditions, we do want to be happy. Is there
anyone here who does not want to be happy in the coming
year? A teacher of a young adult class asked the students to
write their answers to the question, "What do you want most
out of life?" Nine out of ten answered, "Happiness." *Psy-
chology Today* magazine took a poll of 40,000 readers. Eighty-
three percent responded that their main question was, "How
can I find real happiness?"

If anybody should be happy, it is a Christian. But, is the
average Christian known for his joy? Many think of a Christian in terms of solemnity, seriousness, and severity. Some of

us are like the country boy whose grandmother forbade him to engage in "worldly amusements" on Sunday. Dejected and lonely, he walked down to the barn fence and while he was there a mule came up and put his head into the boy's hands. Patting the sad face of the mule, the boy commiserated, "Poor fellow, you must be a Christian, too."

Christians have good reason to be the happiest people in the world. Their happiness is not based upon the condition of the world but upon the condition of the heart. They are happy because of God and not because of man. This is brought out by our text on this first Sunday of the new year: "I will greatly rejoice in the Lord, my whole being shall exult in my God ..." Be happy about what? Be happy in the Lord; rejoice "in my God." And this is no ordinary happiness. The text says, "I will *greatly* rejoice ..." Thus, our text assures us that we can be happy this year regardless of what comes. We can be happy, for one thing, because we are free. Isaiah sings, "He has clothed me with the garments of salvation, he has covered me with the robe of righteousness ..." Isaiah and his people had reason to be happy. God had delivered them from the 50-year bondage of the Babylonians, and now they were back in their own country as a free people. They were saved from their enemies.

As Christians we, too, can be happy because God has set us free through Christ. Contrary to the once-popular song and movie, we are not "Born free." Each of us, according to the Scriptures, is born in slavery to sin and Satan. Since we are conceived and born in sin, we come into the world under the dominion of Satan. This was the definite position of Saint Paul who repeatedly expressed this view in his letters. In fact, the whole creation has fallen under the power of Satan and it groans, waiting for redemption. No one in the slavery of sin can be happy. Each one is miserable with fear, worry, and faced with doom and destruction.

We Christians are the happiest people in the world because Christ has set us free by his death on the cross. This sacrifice on our behalf frees us from the guilt and power of sin. Now we are free from having to earn acceptance with God. There is no longer any problem how to be good enough to be acceptable to God. In his great mercy God in Christ paid the price of our sins and we are free from condemnation and damnation. Because of Christ we are forgiven. Pardon is a gift of grace. As our text says, we are clothed with the robe of righteousness. It is the perfect righteousness of Jesus. Now God does not see us in the nakedness of our sins but sees us covered with the perfection of Christ.

Because of being free from the penalty of our sins, we should be the happiest people on earth. But are we? A teenager once saw a nun in her traditional habit — long black robes and with a sickly pallor on her face. He exclaimed, "Boy, give me my sins!" When a Christian is forgiven his sins, it is like being released from prison. Some years ago a man who was in the Indiana State Prison for 66 years was given his release. Upon getting out and breathing free air again, he told reporters, "I feel like I've just been born again."

This is the way a true Christian feels. He lives daily the happiness of a newly released prisoner, for daily he receives the forgiveness of sins. Because of this he no longer has the fear of future punishment for his sins. As a Christian who has been forgiven, he no longer has to worry about being good enough to please God to get to heaven. He does not have to wonder whether he has done enough good to pass God's final test. He is accepted by God. The door of heaven is open to him. He has the assurance that all is well with his soul. This is what the Psalmist is referring to when he sings, "The joy of thy salvation." A popular gospel song expresses it:

O happy day that fixed my choice
On Thee, my Savior and my God.
Well may this glowing heart rejoice
And shed its raptures all abroad.
Happy Day! Happy Day!
When Jesus washed my sins away.

I'm In Love

A Christian can be happy all the coming year, because, moreover, he is in love. The happiness of a believer is compared to the joy of a bridal couple. In our text we read, "As a bridegroom decks himself with a garland, and as a bride adorns herself with her jewels."

Probably most of you would say that the happiest day of your life was your wedding day. That was the case at the time of the wedding even though it may not be the case later. Gerald Griffin, in his book *The Silent Misery*, claims that 80 percent of our marriages are unhappy.

Nevertheless, we are happy when we are in love. A magazine headline once quoted Phyllis Diller, "It's wonderful to be in love again!" A Christian is in love with Jesus. We are married to God through Jesus. Marriage is a sacred covenant in which two people promise love and loyalty to each other. When we become Christians we, too, enter into a covenant with God. It is made at our baptism, confirmed at our confirmation, and renewed every time we receive the Holy Communion with repentance and faith. Paul speaks of the church as the bride of Christ. As members of the church, we are the bride of Christ, married to Christ, and we are in love with him. We are in love with him, because he first loved us. While we are despicable sinners not lovable or worthy of any consideration, he died for us to make us his very own. Like Hosea, Christ found us in the filth of prostitution of unbelief and brought us out of bondage that we might be his, live under him in his kingdom, and serve him always. In genuine happiness, we can sing, "I'm in love, I'm in love!"

Why does being in love with Christ make us happy? It is because of what love means. If Jesus loves us, it means that we share life with him. Love means that we think the world of each other. You can be happy that Christ knows you and owns you. He would miss you when absent because you are precious to him. A pastor tells the story about his having had a dog named Jiggs when he was a child. He liked to play with

70

Jiggs but not to take care of him. After some years Jiggs became old and ill. One day his mother took the dog to a vet, but Jiggs never came home again for he died there. His mother did not say anything about the dog, and after four days the boy noticed that Jiggs was missing. He confesses that he does not know whether he was shocked over the death of Jiggs or over the fact that he did not miss the dog. That is not the way it is with Jesus. He loves you so much that he misses you: "The Master is here and calls for you."

Because he loves you, he understands your problems. You do not have to suffer or walk alone in this world. Because he was tempted and suffered, he understands what you must endure. It is said that King George IV had an impediment in his speech. It was worse than a stutter. One day he was shown a film studio. The engineer who showed him around had the same difficulty and was embarrassed about it. In his tension he became worse and worse. Finally, the king put his hand on his shoulder and said, "It's all right, friend. I know what it's like."

Not only does Jesus understand our problems, he also walks with us through the world. He promised he would be with us always. Because he loves us, he is with us at all times. In *Crusade In Europe*, General Dwight Eisenhower tells about American troops moving up toward the Rhine River. "We joined some of them and found the troops eager to finish the job . . . Nevertheless, as we walked along I fell in with one young soldier who seemed silent and depressed. 'How are you feeling, son?' I asked. 'General,' he said, 'I'm awful nervous. I was wounded two months ago and just got back from the hospital. I don't feel so good.' 'Well,' I said to him, 'You and I are a good pair, then, because I'm nervous, too . . . Maybe if we just walk along together to the river, we'll be good for each other.' 'Oh,' he said, 'I mean I was nervous; I'm not anymore. I guess it's not so bad around here.' " As with the disciples on the way to Emmaus, Jesus joins us in our earthly walk and at once we lose our fear.

As a Christian you can be happy because you are in love with Jesus. Because of his love, he takes care of you just as a husband takes care of a wife. This frees you from worry about the material things of life. God will provide for your essential needs. This means that your happiness does not depend upon the amount or quality of things possessed. You are not saying, "I could be happy if I had a new car" or "if I had a diamond ring." Material things just do not mean that much anymore. You are secure and happy in his love, because he will provide what you essentially need.

If you are in love with Christ, you are happy because you belong to him. Love possesses a person and lovers become one. They are happy because they have each other. Separate them and they are lonely and miserable. Now you belong to him and you are somebody. Heretofore, you waited for happiness by trying to be somebody. You wanted status, reputation and prestige. You looked for happiness in prominence. Now you do not have to try to be somebody, because you already are somebody. You are Christ's beloved. You have it "made," and now you are happy in his love. That makes you one of the happiest people in the world regardless of what happens in the world.

Mine Is The Victory

There is another reason why you as a Christian can be happy throughout the coming year. It is because you can say in Christ, "I shall overcome." A Christian lives with a sense of victory over the world. This is taught by our text: "For as the earth brings forth its shoots, and as a garden causes what is sown in it to spring up, so the Lord God will cause righteousness and praise to spring up before all the nations." God's cause of righteousness is sure to prevail just as nature each spring comes to life again after the barren winter.

This simply means to say that a Christian is happy even when things are bad, when life is in the winter season. To be a Christian does not guarantee that skies will always be blue

72

and the highways of life will be flower-strewn. Like every other person in the world, a Christian experiences the seamy side of life with disappointments, sorrows, tragedies, injustices, and misunderstandings. Suffering and death come to a Christian as well as to the non-Christian. The difference is that a Christian lives with a spirit of "I shall overcome." In the darkest hour of his life when he was faced with the cross, Jesus said to his Disciples, "In the world you will have tribulation, but be of good cheer, for I have overcome the world."

Happiness comes from a confidence in God's overruling providence. Christians go through life with trust in these words, "All things work together for good to them that love God ..." God can take the worst and change it into the best for us. One day a lady showed the great artist, John Ruskin, a very expensive handkerchief which was ruined by an indelible ink spot that had fallen on it. When Ruskin asked for it, the lady wondered what he would want with a ruined piece of cloth. Some days later he brought it back to her. Starting with the ink blot as a center, Ruskin worked out a beautiful pattern and design. The handkerchief was now more beautiful than ever. That is what God does with our blunders. Knowing this, we are happy to have a God like that.

In his mercy God takes the unfortunate things that befall us and make us better persons out of them. Years ago two music lovers were together listening to recorded music. One of them asked the other to judge which of two playings was better. The first time he used a steel needle. Then he used a thorn. The friend chose the second playing, for it was softer and more tender. A man who heard this story found great comfort in it, because he was suffering from a thorn in the flesh. When he knew that God was using the torn to make him a more understanding and tender person, he could accept his thorn with grace.

True Christians go through life with smiles on their faces. They have a radiance that will not go away no matter what happens. They can even laugh at death, even when their dearest dies. How can this be? It is because as Christians they see beyond death and the grave to life and the resurrection. Christ conquered death, and because Christ lives, those in Christ live, too. This turns a Christian funeral into a victory celebration.

You know, if you and I follow the guidance of our text on this first Sunday of a new year, we can have the happiest year of our lives. This is based on the fact that God is with us and for us. In the coming year God is going to do something good for us. Because of the "Happy Day" when Jesus came into our lives, we can have a "Happy New Year." As Christians we enter the new year with joyful anticipation, excitement and with high hopes for the very best.